Read All About

CATS

by Jaclyn Jaycox

PEBBLE
a capstone imprint

Read All About It is published by Pebble, an imprint of Capstone.
1710 Roe Crest Drive
North Mankato, Minnesota 56003
www.capstonepub.com

Library of Congress Cataloging-in-Publication Data is available on the Library of Congress website
ISBN 978-1-9771-2528-6 (library binding)
ISBN 978-1-9771-2538-5 (eBook PDF)

Summary: Did you know cats sleep around 15 hours a day? Have you heard they can make about 100 different sounds? Find out all about cats' senses, life cycles, behavior, and more in this fact-filled book.

Image Credits
Shutterstock: 4clover, (watercolor) Cover, design element throughout, 5 second Studio, top right 14, Africa Studio, middle right 29, Alexey Kozhemyakin, bottom right 14, Alina Simakova, 16, Ambiento, middle left 9, Andrew Ivan, bottom left 10, Andrey Stratilatov, top 27, Angela Kotsell, top left 26, ANURAK PONGPATIMET, 12, top left 29, Bartkowski, bottom left 13, bmf-foto.de, 24, Chendongshan, top 15, top 25, Chris Mirek Freeman, bottom 31, DenisNata, middle left 21, didesign021, bottom 30, Edwin Butter, top right 6, Elya Vatel, bottom 15, Eric Isselee, top right 10, top left 17, Erik Lam, 4, Ermolaev Alexander, middle left 18, bottom right 18, fantom_rd, top right 23, Fesus Robert, middle left 14, Impact Photography, top 31, Jemastock, design element, Kasefoto, 8, top left 11, Kelvin Degree, design element, Kolomenskaya Kseniya, bottom right 9, Konjushenko Vladimir, bottom left 17, Konstanttin, top right 26, Krissi Lundgren, middle right 11, Kuttelvaserova Stuchelova, bottom right 21, Lainea, bottom left 11, MaxyM, bottom 27, Michael Potter11, middle left 5, Milles Studio, top 30, Natalia Belotelova, top right 9, Nejron Photo, bottom left 6, New Africa, bottom right 7, Nils Jacobi, bottom Cover, top right 21, Nneirda, top 22, Oleksandr Lytvynenko, middle right 17, 28, Ondrej Chvatal, bottom right 5, Osaze Cuomo, middle left 23, panuwat phimpha, bottom 25, Panyawatt, top right Cover, Pavel Shlykov, bottom right 19, Peter Wollinga, 1, PHOTOCREO Michal Bednarek, bottom right 23, Playa del Carmen, bottom left 29, Popova Valeriya, bottom left 5, Rashid Valitov, top left 13, ReVelStockArt, design element, rukxstockphoto, middle right 13, s_derevianko, 20, schankz, bottom 22, Scorpp, middle 13, Sergey Zaykov, top 7, Shawna and Damien Richard, middle right 18, Sonsedska Yuliia, top left 18, Svineyard, bottom 26, Tsekhmister, bottom right 13, turlakova, top right 19, Ukki Studio, top left 19, Volonoff, design element throughout

Editorial Credits
Designer: Kayla Rossow; Media Researcher: Morgan Walters;
Production Specialist: Katy LaVigne

Printed and bound in China
PO3322

Table of Contents

Words in **bold** are in the glossary.

Chapter 1

History of Cats

Cats have been around for thousands of years. People used to think they were sacred. Let's find out more about the history of these furry **felines**.

There are more than 600 million cats in the world.

Scientists believe cats came from North African wildcats.

All cats belong to the same **species**, called *Felis catus*.

lion

Lions, tigers, and leopards are related to cats.

tiger

leopard

Cats are mammals. Mammals breathe air. They give birth to live young.

Cats were first drawn to humans living on farms. There were lots of mice around to catch!

In ancient Egypt, people dressed cats in jewels.

The United States Post Office hired cats in the late 1800s to keep mice away.

Cats became popular indoor pets when cat litter was invented in 1947.

Chapter 2

Cat Breeds

There are many **breeds** of cats. Breeds have different sizes and colors. Each breed has special features.

The International Cat Association recognizes 71 different cat breeds.

There are six breeds of hairless cats.

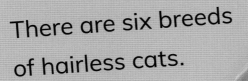

Designer cats come from two different **purebred** parents. Each parent is a different breed.

Savannah is a type of designer breed. Some sell for as much as $30,000!

Maine coons are one of the most popular cat breeds.

American shorthairs are one of the best breeds for hunting mice.

The Abyssinian is one of the oldest cat breeds.

The Singapura is the smallest breed. Some weigh only 4 pounds (2 kilograms)!

British shorthair cats have blue fur.

Chapter 3

Life Cycle

Cats go through different stages of life. Playful kittens become loving cats. Let's see how they grow and change.

Cats go through six stages of life: kitten, junior, prime, mature, senior, and geriatric.

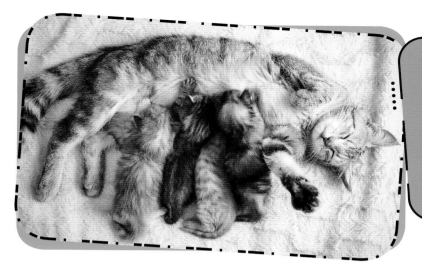

Females give birth to an average of three to five kittens in each litter.

Kittens don't open their eyes until they are one to two weeks old.

All kittens are born with blue eyes. Only a few breeds have blue eyes as adults.

The first six months of a cat's life is equal to 10 human years!

Cats are full-grown between 1 and 2 years old.

On average, cats live about 15 years.

Cats are adults when they reach the prime stage.

Cats are most playful during the kitten stage.

The oldest cat ever lived to be 38 years old.

Chapter 4

Cat Bodies

Each cat looks different. But their bodies are mostly the same. They are purr-fectly designed to be great hunters.

Compared to their body size, cats have the biggest eyes of any mammal.

A cat's tail helps it balance.

Cats have about 250 bones in their bodies. Humans have only 206 bones.

Adult cats have 30 teeth.

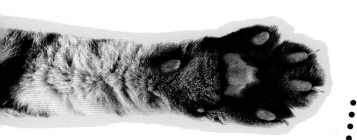

Cats have five toes on each of their front paws. Each back paw has four toes.

Only female cats can have three or more colors in their fur.

A cat's tongue has little hooks on it. The hooks brush the cat's fur when it licks itself.

Cats sweat only through their paws.

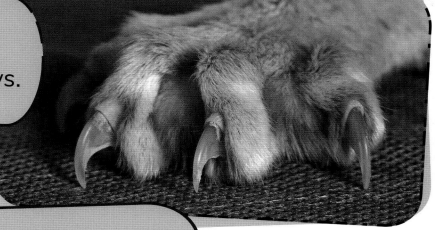

A cat's front claws can **retract**.

Chapter 5

Senses

Cats' **senses** help them explore the world.
Some cat senses are stronger than a human's.
They help cats survive in the wild.

Cats are color blind. Some people believe cats can see only blue and gray.

Cats can see in darkness six times better than humans.

Cats hear much better than humans and even dogs.

* Every cat has a different nose print.

Cats can smell 14 times better than humans.

Cats don't have a strong sense of taste. They can't taste sweet foods at all.

A cat's whiskers are very sensitive. They can feel very small temperature changes.

Cats are nearsighted. It's hard for them to see objects that are far away.

Cats have a blind spot. They can't see things right under their noses.

Chapter 6

Cat Behavior

Have you ever wondered what a cat is thinking? Watching a cat's behavior could give you the answer. Find out what their sounds and actions mean.

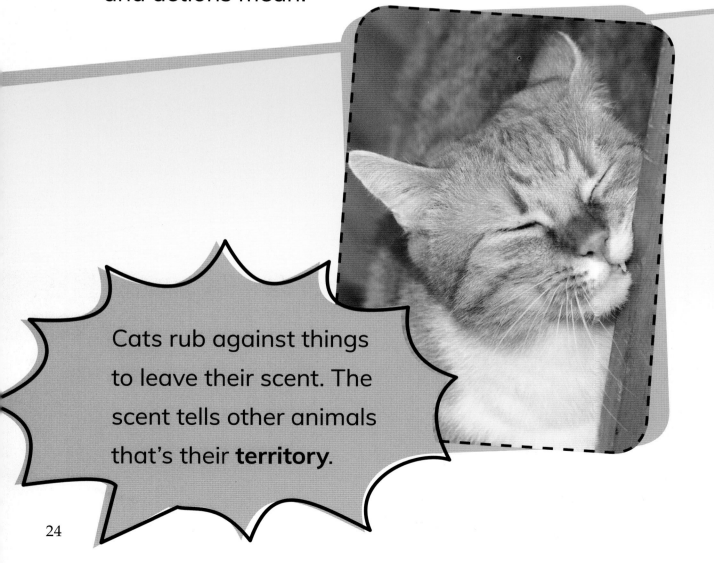

Cats rub against things to leave their scent. The scent tells other animals that's their **territory**.

Cats can make around 100 sounds. Dogs only make about 10 sounds.

Cats don't meow at other cats. They only meow at humans.

A cat's purr can mean it's happy. But cats also purr to calm themselves if they are stressed.

Cats can make different facial expressions.

Cats copy the sounds that birds make.

If a cat wraps its tail around you, the cat is giving you a hug!

Female cats may bring caught mice to their owners. They are being motherly by providing food.

Cats sleep an average of 15 hours a day!

Chapter 7

Caring for Your Pet

Cats make awesome pets. There is a lot to know about taking care of them. It's important to keep them safe, happy, and healthy!

More people have cats as pets than dogs in the United States.

More than 47 million families in the U.S. have a cat.

Cats need fresh water and food every day. A small number of treats is OK too!

Cats should have their litter boxes cleaned every day.

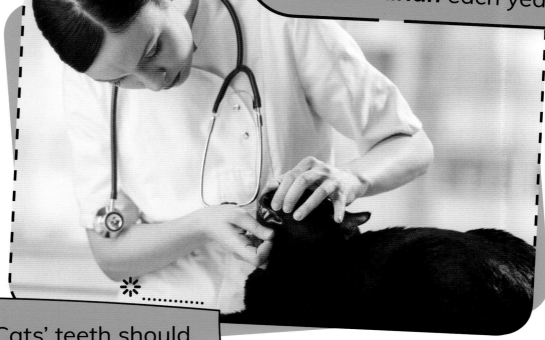

Cats should visit a **veterinarian** each year.

Cats' teeth should be kept clean.

Cats should have **vaccinations** to keep them healthy.

Cats usually keep themselves clean. But be sure to brush their fur!

A cat should wear a collar with an ID tag and bell when going outside.

Glossary

breed—a group of animals that look and act alike

feline—of the cat family

purebred—having parents of the same breed

retract—slide in or out

sense—a way of knowing about your surroundings; hearing, smelling, touching, tasting, and sight are the five senses

species—a group of animals with similar features

territory—an area of land

vaccination—a medicine given to help prevent a certain illness

veterinarian—a doctor trained to take care of animals

Index